Patriarchal Longevity in the Antediluvian Age

By

Samuel Martin

STUDIES IN GENESIS SERIES

Volume Two

This volume is dedicated to my two daughters, Jessica and Christine. May you both live long happy, healthy lives. In Jesus' Name. Amen.

Recompense to no man evil for evil. Provide things honest in the sight of all men.

If it be possible, as much as lieth in you, live peaceably with all men.

Dearly beloved, avenge not yourselves, but rather give place unto wrath:

for it is written, Vengeance is mine; I will repay, saith the Lord.

Therefore if thine enemy hunger, feed him; if he thirst, give him drink:

for in so doing thou shalt heap coals of fire on his head.

Be not overcome of evil, but overcome evil with good. - Romans 12:17-21

© Copyright 2021 by Samuel Martin

Cover design and interior formatting by Dara Stoltzfus

First Edition – Winter 2021

Samuel Martin
Email: info@biblechild.com
Website: www.biblechild.com

ISBN: 978-0-9785339-2-2

The New
Foundation
for
Biblical
Research
Jerusalem

TABLE OF CONTENTS

INTRODUCTION

Patriarchal Longevity in the Antediluvian Age

One of the most interesting aspects to the early history of humankind concerns the Biblical data showing that certain individuals are identified as having lived lives reaching up to almost 1,000 years of age. We today look at these Biblical texts and wonder if they are true or if they just represent ancient myths that primitive mankind believed in.

In this new research study, we are going to explore this question with a view to illuminating difficult passages of the Holy Scripture. We believe that the LORD has given us all the information that we need within the Scriptures themselves to answer all the questions that we may have on most subjects. Understanding how the Patriarchs mentioned in the Bible who lived during the Antediluvian Age lived to be so old is no exception. We pray that you find this publication valuable in your Bible study.

Samuel Martin – Jerusalem, Winter 2021

1

The Theological Orientation of this Book

I was raised in a conservative Bible believing home. Of course, when it came to the Bible, its authority, validity, holiness and perfection were never questioned. I am certain many others could agree with such statements, especially those of us who were children of religious scholars and clergy.

While my late father was a clergyman, he was not a pastoral minister. He was much more focused on training other ministers or teaching Biblical studies at the undergraduate and graduate level in a university environment. Therefore, I was brought up believing that there was a God and His Messiah, our Lord Jesus and that He was revealed to man by the agency of the Holy Bible and the indwelling of the Holy Spirit.

God's son, Jesus, the Messiah, plays a central role in all of this and it is through believing in the person of Jesus Himself as one who was God with us, born in Bethlehem, of a virgin, who grew up in Galilee, began preaching when 30 years of age, lived and died for mankind and was, of course, raised from the dead and now is in heaven waiting until God's chosen time to return to earth and set up an everlasting kingdom that one will experience the resurrection to eternal life.

I believe all of these things because of my association with Jesus Christ and my acceptance of the teachings of Christianity found in the Holy Bible. This belief in a person being 'God with us' affects all kinds of other beliefs that I hold as well. This is particularly the case when we look at the stories found in the Bible, specifically its earlier sections. In this regard, the book of Genesis is our primary focus here and the stories in its pages are of prime importance to this discussion.

Genesis is as much a part of Scripture as is any other book of the Bible

As I said, being connected to Jesus and His message and by expressing faith and believing in Him, there are other cognate beliefs that accompany this one. One of these concerns how I look at the information found in the book of Genesis.

While it may seem fantastic to some people to believe that a being created the heavens and the earth and placed humans here, I personally accept the Scriptural account of this story as found in the book of Genesis. In addition to that, I believe that all human beings alive today are descended from two people as the book of Genesis teaches. I know that many other people reading this book will agree with me in this regard, but I think it is important to make these issues clear at the beginning of this research study.

Now my belief, I admit, about Genesis is strongly affected by what Jesus and the New Testament writers said about that book. Let us rehearse some of this information to better contextualize and appreciate this issue.

Genesis: A Foundation of Divine Revelation

Dr. E. W. Bullinger, the compiler of the Companion Bible, referred to Genesis saying (I agree with his assessment precisely):

"Genesis is the seed-plot of the whole Bible. It is essential to the true understanding of its every part. It is the foundation on which Divine Revelation rests; and on which it is built up. It is not only the foundation of all Truth, but it enters into, and forms part of all subsequent inspiration; … Genesis is quoted or referred to *sixty* times in the New Testament; and Divine authority is set like a seal on its historical facts."[1]

One could go into all of the connections that Jesus (and the other New Testament writers) has with the Genesis narratives, but these are well known, and it is not needed to refer to them here beyond what I have mentioned. It is clear Jesus

---

[1] E. W. Bullinger, The Companion Bible, Appendix II - See Matt. 19:4-6;24:37-28; Mark 7:4,10;10:3-8; Luke 11:43-51;17:26-29; Jn. 1:51;7:21;8:44-56

accepted and taught that all of Genesis was Holy Scripture and I believe He was teaching God's truth. The book of Genesis He had reference to is the same one we have reference to today.

Now, we come to the question that this book seeks to address. The Book of Genesis clearly teaches that there were some people in very ancient times that lived to be over 900 years old. How was that possible? It is this question that we will propose to answer in this research study.

2

Why in the Bible Do We Have
Some People Living Very Long Lives?

I first became interested in this issue in 1996. During that year, I had taken on a new approach to Bible study. I called it "Starting at the Beginning with no pre-conceived ideas." This time was one of great discovery for me. I was starting to develop some of my own theological ideas. I had been working directly with my late father (who was an internationally recognized theological scholar) for ten years, who earned a living by writing and researching Biblical subjects and I was now starting to grow, branch out and do some of my own Bible research.

Genesis was where I started on this new 'Beginning" of research. I started right at Genesis 1:1. I was reading lots of ancient scholarly commentaries (many written by ancient and modern rabbis) and I was learning so much about the broad range of opinions about the early chapters of Genesis.

However, something happened one day in the fall of 1996. One day, while working at my father's office, I was talking to a co-worker and we were discussing scientific matters relating to the book of Genesis in fact and the question of the length of the lives of the ancient Patriarchs came up. How in fact did those ancients live to be so old? In the case of one man, named Methuselah, he reached to an age of 969 years! That is quite a lifetime! How was this possible?

So, the question was asked and I decided at that time to try answering it. Ever since this time, I have always appreciated a good question. I have somehow adopted the saying: "With a good question, a good answer is possible!"

What you are going to read in this research study is the fruit of that research which has since been added to over the last 25 years since it was first published in an outline way in October 1996.

3

Understanding the Issue of Biblical Longevity:
Who Are We Talking About?

Why is it that in the Bible we have some people living very long lives? After posing this question, I began to think and study this matter seeking the Biblical answer to this question. After further research, I began to see things in the Scriptures that I had never seen before.

Let us first remember *who* it is that we are discussing here. The Bible points out *who* it was that lived to these extended ages beyond the normal time allotted to mankind according to our modern understandings of these issues.

The following chart will illustrate the individuals we are focusing on in this discussion. Since we are discussing the longevity of people in the Bible, it seems very important to me that, considering the fact that we are given not much information from the book of Genesis, it would seem appropriate to pay very careful attention to the information that we do have.

Person	Age	Event	From year 1
Adam	130	Seth born	130
Seth	105	Enosh born	235
Enosh	90	Kenan born	325
Kenan	70	Mahalalel born	395
Mahalalel	65	Jared born	460
Jared	162	Enoch born	622
Enoch	65	Methuselah born	687
Methuselah	187	Lamech born	874
Adam	930	Adam dies	930
Enoch	365	Enoch dies[2]	987
Seth	912	Seth dies	1042
Lamech	182	Noah born	1056
Enosh	905	Enosh dies	1140
Kenan	910	Kenan dies	1235
Mahalalel	895	Mahalalel dies	1290
Jared	962	Jared dies	1422
Flood decreed			1536
Noah	500	Japhet born	1556
Noah	502	Shem born	1558
Lamech	777	Lamech dies	1651
Methuselah	969	Methuselah dies	1656
Noah	600	The Flood	1656
Noah	950	Noah dies	2006
Abraham Born			2008

The previous chart was taken from the excellent book "Bible Chronology" by Ivan Panin. Mr. Panin also produced a version of the New Testament in the original manuscript order. [Please contact the author for more information.]

The group of people who lived much longer age's closes with Abraham, who lived to be 175. Note that the people's names who appear in Genesis 11:10-29 all lived to be at least 175. We can add to this list Jacob (147), Isaac (180), Joseph (110), Moses (120), Aaron (123) and Miriam (126 or 127)[3] and a few of Levi's descendants who all lived over 130 years of age (Exodus 6).

---

[2] Hebrews 11:13 states that the previously referenced persons including Enoch died.
[3] http://www.chabad.org/library/article_cdo/aid/112070/jewish/Aaron-and-Miriam.htm

Now that we are clear as to whom we are discussing, we should know what data the Bible supplies to us. The Bible shows that up until the time of Moses, that certain males are recorded as having lived very long lives. The longest lived man was Methuselah who according to divine revelation lived 969 years and then he died.[4] A year in the Bible is defined the length of time it takes the earth to orbit the sun once.[5] Ideally, we see the term "time" used to refer to a year.[6] What the Bible appears to be teaching in this regard is simply this: that a man named Methuselah was born, just as are you and I today, and he lived a period of time that is equivalent to the time it takes the earth to go around the sun 969 times. This is extraordinary from our perspective today and many people in looking at this matter have suggested that the Bible is just relaying primitive myths which have no basis in historical fact. But is this true?

Since we are here entering into a historical question, we have already reviewed the time period under discussion as referenced in our previous table. To be clearer though, what we are specifically speaking about is a time period in human history from the time when Adam was created until the time of the death of Moses in year 2576.[7]

---

[4] Genesis 5:27
[5] Genesis 1:14
[6] Revelation 12:14
[7] Ivan Panin, Bible Chronology, pg. 85

I must also point out *where* these events that we are here speaking of took place. The Bible shows that the descendants of Seth (see Genesis 5 through 37) are the people with whom we are primarily concerning ourselves. These people originated in the land of Mesopotamia. The fact that the Shemites, whose line is traced through Seth back to Adam, remained near the Garden of Eden is important if we want to understand the symbolism in Genesis. I will show why this is so important shortly.

To better understand this geographical information, we must see where the Garden of Eden itself was located.[8] The Garden of Eden was a district located with the land of Eden which was located in ancient Mesopotamia near the northern end of the Persian Gulf.

Now that we know where Eden was, let us understand that it was from this region where the children of Shem had their roots. 'The Shemites dwelt chiefly in Western Asia Minor, south of the Asiatic Japhetites".[9] This is the old region of Eden which later became known as Shinar, the region where the languages were confused. "Shinar" itself is later known to have been located very near to Babylon (*ibid.* pg.95)

---

[8] See Appendix One – Quotation from "Solving the Riddle of Noah's Flood" by Dr. Ernest L. Martin – pgs. 12-14.
[9] Anglican Bible Commentary, Vol. I, pg. 94

Now let us examine the question of why it was that these men were able to live such long-life spans. In my research, I examined the various opinions of rabbis, scholars and theologians who had postulated many diverse theories concerning how some Bible personalities attained such great ages.

To begin, I must remark that there have always been individuals who have attacked the Biblical account of the length of the lives of some of the Patriarchs in the first 2,500 years of human existence as totally absurd and mythical. This view is rampant today and is not new. Various attempts have also been made by some scholars to understand these anomalous accounts by reading a different meaning into the text. It has been suggested that what Moses means in this account is to reckon the years as lunar, not solar. "Some, however, have supposed that the years [of the Patriarchs] above named are lunar, consisting of about thirty days; but this supposition, with a view to reduce the lives of the antediluvians to our standard, is replete with difficulties. At this rate, the whole time from the creation to the Flood would not have been more than 140 years; and Methuselah himself would not have attained to the age which many even now do, whilst many must have had children when mere infants!"[10] Augustine in *'The City of God'* pointed this out as well. (XV.12)

---

[10] M'clintock & Strong, Cyclopedia of Biblical, Theological and Ecclesiastical Literature [CBTEL], vol. V, p. 498.

Abarbanel, a rabbi of the Middle Ages, in his commentary on Genesis 5 'states that some, professing Christianity, had fallen into the same mistake, viz. that Moses meant lunar, and not solar years." (CBTEL, vol. V, p. 499) A similar view appears from the early Christian ecclesiastical historian, Lactantius; "The life of man, though temporary, was yet extended to 1,000 years; of this Varro is so ignorant that, though known to all from the sacred writings [of the Bible] he would argue that the 1,000 years of Moses were, according to the Egyptian mode of calculation, only 1,000 months" (*ibid.*) Irenaeus also points out that no person reached the 1,000 year mark (*Against Heresies*, book 5) He saw in this a fulfillment of a prophecy that no person would reach 1,000 years of life (see I Peter 3:19 and Psalm 90:4 as well as Jubilees 2:24).

Jewish scholars have generally received the ideas that the length of the years in these passages refers to solar years, the year we are familiar with today. Josephus, the Jewish historian of the first century, believed that those years were solar ones, not lunar. "let no one, upon comparing the lives of the ancients with our lives, and with the few years which we now live, think that what we say of them is false, or make the shortness of our lives at present an argument that neither did they attain so long a life" (Antiquities of the Jews, I.3,9). Josephus believed that the years of the ancients equaled our years and many scholars since that time have followed his reasoning in this regard.

There were differences of opinion surrounding the question of whether or not *all* people at this time lived long ages. Rambam (Rambam is an acronym for Rabbi Moses ben Maimon [Maimonidies]) takes the view that only a select group lived a long life and with this view Abarbanel concurs, but Ramban (Rabbi Moses Ben Nachman [Nachmanadies]) disagrees pointing out that, while Moses does not record the ages of the Cainites, there were only seven of them numerated until the Flood [this he supposes] while 10 of the Sethites, whose ages are given, are catalogued before the time of the Flood (*CBTEL*, vol. V, p.499) On the question of whom the longevity applied to, scholars are divided.

After studying this matter, I find myself agreeing with Maimonides. I think and am suggesting that only a select group of people lived long lives.

Let us now consider the evidence that demonstrates this. It is my view that we can now say with some certainty that when the Bible says these men lived over 900 years as we understand the term "year" today, it means that exactly. A year to them was the same as it is to us.

To begin this discussion, I believe that there are two principles that one must have in mind, in my view, when interpreting Genesis. First, on needs to understand that it was substantially edited and compiled by Moses. Jesus said this in Luke 24:44,45 as did Ezra in Malachi 4:4. Without this understanding, one may be in the dark regarding Genesis.

Second, one must also ask what was the reason for writing Genesis in the first place? It appears to me that Moses was giving the Israelites of his time an introduction to the system he was introducing in the wilderness. It is this Mosiac system that can perhaps help us to better understand the earlier parts of Genesis.

4

Temple Symbolism in Genesis

We have referred to the fact that the early sections of Genesis describing the land of Eden and the Garden of Eden were all written or compiled by Moses. These sections have great symbolic teachings to them. These teachings have as their symbolic focus the Holy Temple that was first a tent built by Moses and his contemporaries and later built finally in Jerusalem as a majestic building constructed by Solomon. These early texts in Genesis are full of symbolic teachings if we keep this issue in mind.[11] Let us now review some of these symbolic teachings.

Now, when we start to look at the issues surrounding Temple symbolism in Genesis, it makes good sense to refer to an article written by my late father, Dr. Ernest L. Martin, which brings out these points in a clear way. He noted that:

"It was as if God's celestial palace temporarily had come to earth. Even the Garden, the Cherubim of the Garden, the altar built by Cain and Abel, the land

---

[11] For more information, please see the paper "Temple Symbolism in Genesis" by Ernest Martin, FBR 1977.

of Eden, and the land of Nod are all connected with the temple symbolism and are direct images of God's heavenly abode."[12]

The first point we wish to discuss concerns the issue of the language used to describe the various times when the LORD and Adam and Eve had contact. Note the following: "In the Garden our first parents were able to talk face to face with the LORD. But note an important point. They only had conversations with Him at certain times of the day. They did not see Him on all occasions. It was "in the cool of the day" that they came into "the presence of the LORD" (Gen. 3:8). The expressions "cool of the day" and "the presence of the LORD" were a part of the language associated with the Temple. "The cool of the day" was the period when the sun got lower in the sky and the cool sea breezes normally swept over Israel. This was the time of the evening sacrifice (I Kings 18:36; Daniel 9:21) about three in the afternoon. ... At these times the people were then reckoned as being "in the presence of God" (II Chronicles 20:19)."[13]

Note also that the incident where the heavenly beings, the Cherubim, are mentioned in the early section of Genesis and how this relates to Temple symbolism. "So he drove out the man; and he placed at the east of the garden of Eden Cherubim, and a flaming sword which turned every way, to keep the way of the tree of life" (Genesis 3:22-24). This episode has some very significant

[12] Ernest Martin, Temple Symbolism in Genesis: Foundation for Biblical Research: 1977
[13] Ernest Martin, Temple Symbolism in Genesis: Foundation for Biblical Research: 1977

features associated with it. Observe that they were expelled east of the Garden. Cherubim (angelic beings - later connected with temple symbolism) were also stationed at the east gate to the Garden with a flaming sword to prevent Adam and Eve from re-entering.[14] The Cherubim guarded the east entrance (the only gate) into the Garden and forbade anyone to enter. We will see in a moment that these features represent precise arrangements found in the later tabernacle and temples."[15]

The Genesis narrative relates to the Garden of Eden and is full of Temple Symbolism

When we look at the whole narrative of Genesis, we find the following parallels which are given in Genesis and relate to other sections of the Bible related to the Temple. It is really quite important to understand that the information in the early sections of Genesis has a clear "Temple" orientation to it. Without an agreement with this point, one will face serious challenges accepting the thesis herein outlined. Let us just give a short summary here.[16]

---

[14] A question we have to ask here concerns the issue of whether these cherubim ever permitted Adam back into the Garden? Based upon Temple Symbolism, we might find that certain persons just might have allowed in only on one specific day.

[15] ibid.

[16] For a more detailed examination of these points, see: Martin, Temple Symbolism in Genesis: Foundation for Biblical Research: 1977 and the book Secrets of Golgotha (2nd Edition: ASK Pubs, 1996) which has several sections which discuss these points.

Temple Type in Genesis	Temple Anti-Type
1. The Inner Garden[17]	The Holy of Holies[18]
2. The Larger Garden[19]	The Holy Place[20]
3. Cain and Abel's Altar[21]	The Altar of Burnt Offering[22]
4. Eden[23]	The Camp of Israel[24]

---

[17] "The Book of Jubilees stated that the inner "Garden" was analogous to the sanctuary in the Temple (Jubilees 8:19 and compare Jub. 3:10-12)." (Martin, Secrets of Golgotha: ASK Pubs: 1996, p. 238); See also Gen. 3:3 talking about the "midst of the garden."

[18] "The Holy Place of the Temple into which only the priests could enter to perform their administrations was acknowledged as "the Garden" section of the Land of Eden. This was where Adam and Eve lived at first before they sinned. Further inside "the Garden" was an inner part to which God would appear at specified times. This was like the Holy of Holies." (*ibid.*); See also Exodus 26:33 & Numbers 7:89.

[19] "These matters [noted in footnotes 17 & 18] are good evidence to show that this "Garden" area was represented by the Holy Place in the Temple of Solomon." (*ibid.*)

[20] "The Bible records that Solomon "carved all the walls of the house [the Holy Place] round about with carved figures of cherubim and palm trees and open flowers within and without" [that is, the carvings were on the inside walls of the Holy Place as well as on its outside walls] (I Kings 6:29; see also Ezekiel 41:18 where the prophet also decorated his future, prophetic Temple in the same way)." (*ibid.*)

[21] "It was only in the "Garden" section of Eden that they could no longer enter. And then, sometime later their two sons Cain and Abel built an altar. This was positioned before the entrance to "the Garden" (in which God was supposed to dwell)." (*ibid.* pgs.238-239); See also Genesis 4:4,5.

[22] "Concerning the sacred furniture in the Tabernacle and Temple this altar was analogous to the Altar of Burnt Offering which was positioned just east of the entrance to the Holy Place [or "the Garden"]." (*ibid.* pg. 239)

[23] Genesis 2,3 & 4; See also

[24] Deuteronomy 23:11,13,14

Temple Type in Genesis	Temple Anti-Type
5. The Land of Nod[25]	Outside the Camp of Israel[26]
6. The Altar for Cain[27]	The Miphkad Altar[28]
7. City of Cain[29]	Cities of Refuge[30]

Now, in orienting ourselves to this Temple type/anti-type, we can now start to better put the flesh on the skeleton of how certain of the ancient Patriarchs could have lived such long lives.

---

[25] "But Cain killed Abel. This forced Cain to move east of Eden (Gen.4: 16). This signaled that Cain and his descendants could no longer live in the Land of Eden. They had to remain eastward of "Eden" in the Land of Nod (Wandering)." (*ibid.*); See also this author's book "What was the Mark of Cain?") "So what does this mean relative to the use of the phrase "land of Nod" in Genesis 4:16? It has a great deal to do with it, because perhaps what the intended meaning here is not the "land of wandering," but rather the **"land of mourning."**
- www.amazon.com/gp/product/0978533917/ref=dbs_a_def_rwt_bibl_vppi_i3
[26] Numbers 2 & Hebrews 13:13
[27] "While east of Eden and in the Land of Nod, God promised Cain a sacrifice for sin if he ever did wrong. God said to Cain: "if you do not well, sin [a sin offering] couches at the door" (Gen.4:7). The couching of this sin offering for Cain meant (in the usage of the word in other contexts of the Bible) that it would be so weighted down with "sin" that it would have to couch at the door because of the heavy weight. Before what door was this sin offering placed? Since all sin offerings had to be presented "in the presence" of God for acceptance (and since God dwelt in inner sanctum of "the Garden" in the Land of Eden), Cain's sin offering was prophesied to couch before the door represented the eastern gate to the Land of Eden." (*ibid.* pg. 239)
[28] "In Tabernacle and Temple this altar on which Cain's sin offering would be placed by the Miphkad Altar located on the Mount Olives and outside the Temple (even outside the camp of Ezekiel 43:21)." (*ibid.* pg. 239)
[29] Genesis 4:17 – This text is shown to refer later to the cities that Moses founded as cities of refuge. See below.
[30] "Indeed, we find also, that the Eastern quarter [in this case, the land of Nod] always forms a place of refuge for murderers, as it is said: (Deut: 4:41) "Then Moses set aside 3 cities of refuge towards the place of sun-rise." Rosenbaum & Silbermann, "Rashi's Commentary on the Pentateuch," p.19. Shapiro/Valentine & Co., London, 1946.

5

Practical Application of the Temple Symbolism in Genesis

It is this key that provided me with the motivation to ask further questions regarding the account of Moses in the book of Genesis. The first question I asked concerned Adam being told to leave the Garden. Here is the question I asked: Does the Bible say in that account that Adam would never ever be permitted to once again enter the Garden for any reason or at any time?

As I thought on this, and remembered that the two regions of the Garden and the land of Eden were analogous to the three compartments of the Temple, it then seems clear to me that, as the High Priest could enter the Holy of Holies on one day during the year (Exodus 30:10), so likewise could not Adam also be afforded the same liberty by God according to Temple symbolism?

Could Adam have been permitted back into the Garden and if so, what would he do given such an opportunity? To me that answer appeared clear. He would walk over to the Tree of Life and eat! Another question also comes to my mind? Did Adam have any seeds from the Tree of Life? He would have certainly understood how trees, plants and animals (as well as human beings) propagated themselves. If God had sent mankind out of the Garden to till the ground, would He not have provided them seeds from the trees in the Garden?

This Tree of Life, which was almost certainly the almond tree (see Numbers 17:8) is referenced in the early narratives of Genesis associated with these Patriarchal figures. Notice that Jacob cultivated and used the almond tree for food (Genesis 43:11). He also considered the almond an appropriate gift to give to the man (who was in fact his son, Joseph) who was in a position right under the Egyptian Pharaoh.

What my research shows is that while Adam (and some of his descendants) were indeed "banished" or "driven out" of the Garden, they were able to reenter the Garden at specific times for specific reasons. In fact, our merciful God allowed certain persons back into the Garden, some for perhaps short intervals like a day, but others for much longer periods of time. Let's look at these issues in greater detail now.

6

The Garden of Eden:

Were Adam and His Descendants Ever Allowed Back In?

When we consider the question of whether or not Adam (or some of his descendants) were ever allowed back into the Garden of Eden, it seems from the biblical text that the quick answer is "no!" Let us review here the key text in question in this regard.

"Therefore the LORD God sent him forth from the garden of Eden, to till the ground from whence he was taken. So he drove out the man; and he placed at the east of the garden of Eden Cherubim, and a flaming sword to keep the way of the tree of life." (Genesis 3:23-24)

This text seems very clear and there appears to be a distinct finality to it. When we combine this text with the following previous verse, we can receive some additional information. Note it here:

"And the LORD God said, Behold, the man is become as one of us, to know good and evil: and now, lest he put forth his hand, and take also of the tree of life, and eat, and live forever." (Genesis 3:22)

While it seems from this verse that Adam and Eve had not yet eaten of the tree of life, it seems that there was no prohibition to them doing so based upon the LORD's earlier statements in Genesis 3:16, where the explicit permission to "Of every tree of the garden, thou mayest freely eat: …" In addition, the text clearly shows that eating of that tree could cause life to be extended. Note though that when we see the word "forever" (Hebrew: *olam*), we must note that this word does not necessarily denote eternity. Refer in this regard to the following: "the word or phrase translated "eternal, forever, or forever and ever" come from the Hebrew word *olam* or the Greek word *aeon* and they mean an indefinite length of time but always with a beginning and an ending. Indeed, in the case of Jonah, he was in the belly of the fish for three days and nights but in 2:6 the King James translators rendered the time period as "forever." The words really mean "age" and "age-lasting" and should be consistently translated in that fashion or something similar."[31]

So, when we note these texts, Adam was indeed sent out of the Garden of Eden and his access to the tree of life was indeed restricted in some sense, but the important thing to note about this whole issue is that Adam and some of his descendants lived lives that far exceeded the life expectancies that we today are familiar with or were even characteristic of full lives in Biblical times.

---

[31] Dr. Ernest L. Martin, The Biblical Manual, Chapter 8

We note that the Bible gave the normal life expectancy for a full life of seventy years with the example of King David. However, Adam and some of his descendants are recorded to have lived over 900 years in several cases. One person, Methuselah, lives to be 969 years. But how?

This phenomenon, as you will carefully note in this book, was not a universal phenomenon. It was something that was limited to a select group of people and in this regard we can point precisely to the direct descendants of Adam and the individuals referenced in the book of Genesis up until the time of Abraham, who reached 175 years of age reaching down to the parents of Moses and Aaron (who lived 120 and 123 years respectively). What we see with the biblical record is that this line of extreme longevity when it came to age follows a path that leads to the first High Priest of the nation of Israel, Aaron. After that, we do not read of hardly anyone who surpassed the age of 100.

What does this have to do with the issue of whether or not Adam and some of his descendants were ever allowed back into the Garden of Eden? It has much to do with it because the Garden of Eden was modeled according to a particular design which was manifested later when the Solomon's Temple was built and which was earlier modeled in the ancient Tabernacle which served as God's residence while He lived with the people of Israel.

In an article titled "Temple Symbolism in the book of Genesis," which my late father wrote and which research has been reproduced in numerous other

Bible studies and books that he published which showed that there existed compartments or different areas of the Garden of Eden. There was the inner garden and the whole of the Garden itself and then the Garden itself was located in the land of Eden. Then, when Cain sinned and was banished from Eden, he went into Nod (the land of Mourning – as I have shown in my book "What was the Mark of Cain?") Even in Nod, which was also a large area, there was a specific place for the Altar for Cain and for the city that he founded.

All of these geographical points have their exact counterparts in the geography and organizational layout of the Tabernacle and Temple structures. These can be characterized as follows:

Type	Anti-Type
The Inner Garden of Eden	The Holy of Holies
The Garden of Eden itself	The Holy Place
Eden	The Camp of Israel
The land of Nod	Outside the Camp of Israel
The Altar for Cain in Nod	The Miphkad Altar (Leviticus 4:1-21)
The City of Cain	City of Refuge mentioned by Moses

Now, considering that this model is easily demonstrated from the Bible and from ancient Jewish sources, when we look at the early Genesis narrative and start to put some flesh on the skeleton which is here given, we can note some specific aspects of Mosiac legislation which may very well have application to our story here in Genesis and this has direct bearing on the issue of longevity of age and on the ability of Adam and some of his direct descendants who were able to periodically reenter not only the Garden of Eden, but even to go directly into the very inner part of the Garden where they were seemingly forever forbidden to enter. How can this be? When you think about it, it is quite simple.

The key to this whole issue is the legislation that Moses proposed concerning that holiest day of the Hebrew calendar: the Day of Atonement or in the original Hebrew, the day of covering. (see Leviticus 23:27,28) Note here the ritual that took place on that day and what it involved:

"Only on the DAY OF ATONEMENT, when he was required to atone for the sins of the entire nation, did the High Priest enter the Holy of Holies. He prepared for this moment by separating himself from his family a week in advance and remaining inside the Temple. He purified himself physically and spiritually and reviewed all the laws pertaining to his service. On the Day of Atonement, as part of a day of fasting, offering sacrifices, and confession of sins, the High Priest entered the Holy of Holies. He placed two handfuls of incense on a pan of burning coals, and as the smoke filled the chamber, the Divine Presence was revealed and the nation of Israel forgiven for its sins" (Yoma 5:1).

31

[Note that YOMA is one of the tractates from the Babylonian Talmud.]

Isn't it interesting that on a certain day there even referenced in Genesis that Adam and Eve attempted to "cover" themselves due to their sin of eating the forbidden fruit? Later on though, we find the LORD Himself providing what? Coverings (or what we today call clothing) for their physical beings. Could it be that that day when the event of animal skins being provided for Adam and Eve became known in later times as the day of covering (or in Hebrew *yom kippur*)? It certainly looks like that could very well be possible.

We can here also note some comments made by my father on this issue:

"There was one day in the Old Testament which was commanded as a day of affliction: the tenth day of the seventh Jewish month. All people were to be afflicted (be fasting -Ezra 8:21-23] on that day. Rituals were performed to reconcile the ancient Israelites to God because of the sins the nation had committed [both collectively and individually] over the previous year (Leviticus 16:23-25). The fasting was to accent the sorrow they should have had for their demerits.

32

There may also be another reason why the Israelites fasted on that day. Adam and Eve were told they could eat of all of the fruits of the trees in the Garden of Eden except one. Because the trees had fruit on them indicates that the events recorded in Genesis Two occurred in the Autumn. This may well be. Symbolically, the first day of creation (starting with Genesis 1:1) could have been the first day of the Jewish Autumn month called Tishri. The seventh day of creation would answer to the seventh day of Tishri. After that "Sabbath," we find Adam and Eve in the Garden and curious over the various trees and their many fruits. The serpent then tempted Eve to take of the forbidden fruit. She did, along with Adam. Isn't it interesting that this simple eating of some small items of fruit introduced sin into the world? Though the eating was a small thing in one way, it had major consequences. Their eating made them sinners, and now a Savior would have to die on a tree of crucifixion to atone for that sin - and all others of mankind that have since been committed. The consequence was so serious that the serpent was sent on his belly as a curse and Adam and Eve were expelled from the Garden.

Since the seventh day (weekly Sabbath) of creation could symbolically be considered the seventh of the Jewish month Tishri, then it could well be that sin was introduced to the world three days later on Tishri 10 - the very day that later became the Day of Atonement in the time of Moses. This makes perfectly good sense. The serpent introduced sin on that day, so is it not reasonable that sin would also be dealt with in regard to Israel and their Old Covenant relationships with God on that day? And since the first sin involved eating, God could very well have emphasized his abhorrence of sin by commanding the Israelites to abstain from food on that day." (Dr. Ernest Martin – Article – Fasting: Its Use and Abuse, Oct. 1997, FBR.)

The point is, after Adam and Eve had sinned, some new procedures for approaching God were organized and put into action and these procedures were later modified and structured in the Mosaic legislation. These early actions were shadows of future rules which were to regulate the ancient Israelite interactions with the LORD.

And what were some of the rules associated with this "day of covering" or "atonement" as many versions have it? One of them was the allowance of the High Priest of the nation to enter into the Holy of Holies for a certain period of time and offer prayers to God for the nation of Israel. (see earlier reference to YOMA 5:1)

This clear reference provides us here with our key which shows that the LORD even in the biblical period of Genesis going up until the time of the Flood and even after allowed those individuals who were the designated religious representative of the people at that time and who had direct lineage to Adam and had this specific designation of High Priest to enter not only the Garden of Eden, but to enter its most inner part which was analogous to the Holy of Holies in the later Temple built by Solomon. We can know who these individuals were because they are listed in the Bible. (See earlier chart)

Down to the time of Noah, who we certainly must consider fulfilled all of the qualifications of being a High Priest of his family, we can begin to note who became the High Priest after Noah? It was clearly his son Shem and after that, the High Priesthood was transmitted to other people who are listed in Genesis 11:10-29. We can note also that Abraham also has to be considered a type of a High Priest physically speaking and some of his actions clearly demonstrate this.

And what is the single factor that ties these people together? It is their advanced ages. We must once again remember that long life was not mandatory of all and people could be killed (like Abel who was killed by Cain or like even Cain's recognition of the fact that he could be killed at any time) or die from illness or perish in the Flood. All of these facts show that the longevity that certain people had was not universal. No, not at all. That longevity was seemingly reserved for only selected individuals.

The point in this discussion relative to how Adam and some of his descendants were able to periodically re-enter the Garden of Eden goes back to that issue of the geography of Eden and its comparative nature to the various compartments of the Temple of God. If the High Priest was able to enter the

Holy of Holies on one day per year and this compartment of the Temple is analogous to the Inner Garden of Eden, then in like manner on that specific day of the year, a day when the sins of the people were "atoned" for (or as the Hebrew word actually conveys meaning "covering"), whoever was the High Priest at that time (be it Adam or the individual to whom the position of High Priest was transferred) could have entered the Inner Garden of Eden from where he was previously banished.

7

What was the Means Used to Secure the Long Life in the Bible?

When we read in the books of Isaiah and Ezekiel descriptions of the Messianic age we note some interesting points which may indeed have bearing on this question. Isaiah points out that in the Messianic age of the Millennium that children will live to be 100 years old. (Isaiah 65:20) We also read in Ezekiel that there will exist trees beside the river of water that will proceed from the Holy Temple at that time and that these trees will provide food that will change each month and that their leaves will provide medicine (Ezekiel 47:12). If this is the case, we can see that there is something that is keeping these children alive for longer periods than we are used to and there exists something that people can use for medical purposes from these trees that will help them get better. If you have children living over 100 years and have the ability for sick people to get better from medicinal leaves, you have the formula for a universal situation that mirrors what was taking place in the early period of Genesis, only now it will be available more widely than it was previously.

What the text in Ezekiel seems to show is that God uses these miraculous trees to extend life and what did we find in the inner most part of the Garden of Eden? We had a tree of life and those who could eat of it saw their lives extended.

Now, did everyone get to eat of it? No! Did those who could eat of it see their lives extended permanently? No. But, we can say for sure that some people in the ancient world (whose identities and lineage we have here referenced and the context into which their long lives must be placed) did live for very long periods of time and did have their mortal lives extended.

We also note that inside the Holy of Holies where the Ark of the Covenant was kept that one of the items referenced was the Aaron's rod. (Hebrews 9:4) According to the Biblical account, that rod bloomed, had flowers and brought forth almond buds. (a clear symbol of the tree of life [see Jeremiah 1:11] (Num. 17:8) Could it be that while the Temple was in existence and the rod of Aaron occupied its position in the Ark of the Covenant that one of the things that the High Priest did when he went into the Temple was to eat some of the fruit of that miraculous almond tree? Could it be that if God wished the ministry of a particular High Priest extended, He might have permitted that High Priest to eat of that almond rod that had life in itself? We are not told.

What it seems to show is that God allowed these High Priestly individuals to enter the Holy of Holies (which the Inner Garden of Eden of Eden symbolized) on an annual basis and during that time, they could experience a chance to eat from the tree of life which would then extend their mortal lives.

Of course, some might say that the whole suggestion does not seem to make sense particularly considering the seeming finality of the decree of God in

Genesis 3:22-24. Yes, on the surface it does seem to be very final and there seems to be not much room for such an interpretation. However, in researching this issue I noted the following opinion of the Rabbi Yosef Kimchi quoted by Tur, who said the following talking about Genesis 3:23: "the repetition of the verse implies that after man was *sent forth* from the garden, he returned." (Art Scroll Tanach Series, Vol. 1, Bereshis, pg. 140.)

We can also note that many interpretations of these verses (Genesis 3:22-24) exist which do not reflect the literal sense of the verse. Note what Rabbi Solomon Ben Issac (Rashi) in his commentary on the book of Genesis said: "there are Agadic Midrashim [legendary stories], but they [these stories about Genesis 3:22-24] are not in keeping with its (the verse's) plain sense." (Rashi's Commentary on the Pentateuch, Vol. 1, pg. 16; A. Blashki & I. Joseph; Shapiro, Valentine & Co.: 1946.)

This interpretation shows that there were a variety of ideas and interpretations concerning this verse, so maybe my suggestions here make sense.

The Requirement to Fast on the Day of Atonement – A Problem

One of the Biblical teachings concerning the Day of Atonement which has come into practice based on interpretation was that all Israelites were required to fast.

They were not allowed to eat food or drink for just over 24 hours. Traditionally, the text in Leviticus 23:26-32 has meant to abstain from food:

"The Lord spoke to Moses, saying: Now, the tenth day of this seventh month is the day of atonement; it shall be a holy convocation for you: you shall **deny yourselves** and present the Lord's offering by fire; and you shall do no work during that entire day; for it is a day of atonement, to make atonement on your behalf before the Lord your God. For anyone who does not practice **self-denial** during that entire day shall be cut off from the people. And anyone who does any work during that entire day, such a one I will destroy from the midst of the people. You shall do no work: it is a statute forever throughout your generations in all your settlements. It shall be to you a sabbath of complete rest, and **you shall deny yourselves**; on the ninth day of the month at evening, from evening to evening you shall keep your sabbath." (NRSV)

Up until this time, there was no specific Biblical mention of the keeping of the Day of Atonement. It was instituted in the time of Moses.

It is very possible that earlier traditions about the Day of Atonement are alluded to in Scripture and we are referring to some of them here in this present research study. What is important to note though is that while certain teachings were given in the time of Moses like this one we are presently discussing, it is very

40

possible that the rules that governed the matter prior to the time of Moses may have taught completely different things concerning what was taught at later times. Let us look at some very specific examples that make this assertion clear.

Earlier Biblical Teachings that were Changed in the Time of Moses

On the surface, we might imagine that teachings given in the Bible would remain fixed and not change as time went on. We might think that such a teaching makes sense, but if we did not study this matter carefully, we would find out that this is not always the case. God teaches us in a progressive way often changing religious requirements as time goes on or as His priorities change.

This is particularly the case when you study the teachings in the Bible given prior to the time of Moses. What you will find is many earlier teachings which were given in the time of Moses and became a part of God's Holy Law, in prior times, these practices, which later became forbidden, were allowed in the earlier period and were practiced by individuals who were in covenant relationships with God. It might seem mistaken and fantastic to suggest such a thing, but the Bible indicates this on numerous occasions concerning a variety of teachings which as time went on were changed. What was allowed in earlier times became forbidden in later times. Let us review some instances of this idea which the Bible teaches quite directly. In this regard, I want to refer to a booklet written by my late father, Dr. Ernest L. Martin, which really demonstrates this issue well.

"With the introduction of the covenant of circumcision between God and man (specifically with Abraham and his seed), **religious requirements became more ritualistic and distinctive**. But when Moses was commissioned by God to give the Israelites His Old Covenant revelation, **ceremonialism became even more pronounced**. Indeed, **the differences between the patriarchal religious system established in the time of Abraham and that begun in the time of Moses were as different as daylight and dark**. Let's look at the dissimilarities.

Under the Abrahamic covenant, God allowed His people to offer sacrifices anywhere they pleased (Genesis 12:7; 35:1: Job 1:5), but Moses changed this by commanding only the family of Aaron to attend to the sacred rites (Exodus 40:1-16), and those sacrifices could only be offered on the altar in the Sanctuary (Deuteronomy 12:13,14). Abraham planted a grove (or sacred tree) in Beersheba (Genesis 21:33). But under Moses the use of groves became prohibited (II Chronicles 14:3: Isaiah 17:8). Jacob set up a pillar (Genesis 28:18). But this was later forbidden by Moses (Deuteronomy 3:22, margin). God had said in the time of Noah: "Every moving thing i.e., all animals! that liveth shall be meat for vou: even as the green herb have I given you all things" (Genesis 9:3), but with Moses, only the beasts which were mentioned in Leviticus 11 were allowed or disallowed.

42

There were no official feast days commanded in the time of Abraham, but with Moses, the ordained festivals became commanded periods for attendance by all Israelite males (Leviticus 23). Tithing was not a law in the patriarchal period, but with Moses, it became a strict dictate (Deuteronomy 12:11). None of the Patriarchs wore phylacteries (at least we have no record of such), but with Moses. their use was commanded (Numbers 15:37-41) The land did not have to rest every seventh year under the Patriarchs (Genesis 41:34,35), but with Moses, that too was changed (Leviticus 25:1-7). Abraham even married his half-sister with God's approval (Genesis 20:12), but this became illegal in the time of Moses (Leviticus 20:17), Abraham was also confederate with his Canaanite neighbors (Genesis 14:13), but no leagues with the Canaanites were allowed in the dispensation of Moses indeed, the Canaanites were to be exterminated (Deuteronomy 20:17,18). There was also no commanded Sabbath law in the patriarchal period, but in the time of Moses the Sabbath was first introduced as a law (Nehemiah 9:14; Ezekiel 20:12) with many stringent requirements that changed the very character of the seventh day of the week. Moses had now come on the scene and what a profound change in religious essentials occurred.

The differences between the religious system of the Patriarchs and that of Moses were dramatic. Look at it this way. If a religious Israelite in the time of David (well within the Mosaic dispensation) could have been transported back to Abraham's time and witnessed Abraham (not knowing who he was) performing his religious duties, he would no doubt have called him an unconverted heathen. For the first ninety-nine years of Abraham's life, he wasn't circumcised; then later he built altars anywhere he pleased; he raised up groves; he offered no lamb at Passover; he kept no weekly Sabbath; he attended no holy feasts; he wore no phylacteries; he married his half-sister; kept no land sabbath; and of all things, he was allied with the Canaanites.

Actually, **what God did in the time of Moses was to rescind the religious requirements of the patriarchal period in favor of the more strict laws ordained in the time of Moses**. The two religious systems were so completely different from one another that were one to try mixing them together utter confusion would result.

However, there are some people who are so conservative that they will not allow God to bring in new religious systems different from previous ones. They cannot believe that God changes His mind (and He doesn't in overall philosophical matters). But God has most decidedly changed whole religious systems in the past, and these alterations are recorded in the Bible.

God uses the principle of Progressive Revelation throughout the Bible and introduces new and mature systems of worship as best suits Him. The other prime example of this being done is God's change of the Mosaic system into the advanced Christian one. Really, **the diversities between the Mosaic and Christian systems are as pronounced as between the Mosaic and**

Patriarchal. It is important that people begin to comprehend, and to apply, these facts if they ever hope to understand what God now requires of man."[32]

This quote demonstrates quite clearly that it is very possible that in earlier times in the book of Genesis that God may have allowed this priestly patriarchal figure who would have entered the Garden of Eden once per year to have been able to eat of the tree of life on that day and to have his life extended. What happened later in the Day of Atonement rituals, where fasting became a practice required by all, could very well not have even existed in the earlier period.

What we need to understand is that what was taught in earlier times may have changed in later times and the Bible is full of examples of this taking place. Not only that, we can also point out a specific example of a biblical personality, King David, eating something which was dedicated to God and only allowed to be eaten by a certain group of individuals defined by God in His Holy Word.

Eating Holy Food Reserved Only For Priests

Just because a biblical law says something, God can adjust His laws as He sees fit when He wishes to do so. An excellent example of this is found in the story

---

[32] Ernest Martin, Progressive Revelation in the Bible, FBR: Pasadena: CA. 1980

of King David and his colleagues eating the shewbread which was kept in the Holy Tabernacle with the permission of God's Priest. Note I Samuel 21:1-6:

"Then David came to Nob, to Ahimelech the priest. And Ahimelech came to meet David, trembling, and said to him, "Why are you alone, and no one with you?" And David said to Ahimelech the priest, "The king has charged me with a matter and said to me, 'Let no one know anything of the matter about which I send you, and with which I have charged you.' I have made an appointment with the young men for such and such a place. Now then, what do you have on hand? Give me five loaves of bread, or whatever is here." And the priest answered David, "I have no common bread on hand, but there is holy bread—if the young men have kept themselves from women." And David answered the priest, "Truly women have been kept from us as always when I go on an expedition. The vessels of the young men are holy even when it is an ordinary journey. How much more today will their vessels be holy?" So the priest gave him the holy bread, for there was no bread there but the bread of the Presence, which is removed from before the Lord, to be replaced by hot bread on the day it is taken away." (ESV)

King David and his colleagues who were with him ate bread which was reserved for only Aaronic priests! Note the book of Leviticus which makes this fact clear:

"Take the finest flour and bake twelve loaves of bread, using two-tenths of an ephah for each loaf. Arrange them in two stacks, six in each stack, on the table of pure gold before the Lord. By each stack put some pure incense as a memorial portion to represent the bread and to be a food offering presented to the Lord. This bread is to be set out before the Lord regularly, Sabbath after Sabbath, on behalf of the Israelites, as a lasting covenant. It belongs to Aaron and his sons, who are to eat it in the sanctuary area, because it is a most holy part of their perpetual share of the food offerings presented to the Lord." (Lev. 24:5-9 NIV)

The point is, God can make exceptions to His laws whenever He wishes and the Bible makes this plain and clear even though we have direct statements in other sections of Scripture which say that it is not allowed.

**Jesus Allowed His Disciples to Work by Picking Grain
and Eating It On A Sabbath
Referring to King David's Example Eating the Holy Bread in the Temple**

The idea of God changing His earlier laws and permitting them to be broken if He wishes it is reiterated in the teachings and actions of our Lord Jesus Christ while He was in the flesh prior to His crucifixion, death and resurrection from the dead. This is particularly relevant to our present discussion because our Lord

47

Jesus permitted His disciples to break one of His laws written in the Law of Moses, eat food and suffer no negative consequences for that behavior. He even refers to the actions of King David, which we have just mentioned of eating the Holy Bread in the Tabernacle and later Temple which was reserved only for Aaronic priests. This whole matter is explained well in the following quote:

"When Christ's disciples went through the grain fields on the Sabbath, they plucked the grain, rolled it in their hands and ate it. The Pharisees said His disciples were doing "that which is not lawful to do upon the Sabbath day" (Matthew 12:2). And true enough, the activity of the apostles was strictly forbidden by biblical law (Exodus 16:27–30). Sabbath-keeping denominations normally feel that Christ or His disciples did not really break the Sabbath of God. They think that He was simply not concerned over "minor work" being done on that day. But this is not true. Christ was as interested in the smaller points of the law like mint and anise and cummin (Matthew 23:23) as He was in major matters. After all, if one breaks the law even in a minor way, he still breaks the law. But Christ permitted His disciples to break the biblical Sabbath law. And Christ was not a sinner in doing this. He was the Lord of the Sabbath. This is clear in the New Testament.

Note Christ's answers to the Pharisees critical of Him. He did not say: "God never meant that the gathering of a few handfuls of grain is Sabbath-breaking." No, He said nothing like that. Christ admitted that His disciples had truly broken the Old Testament Sabbath law. And Christ, as an excuse for His disciples, gave the Pharisees some illustrations of how others in the past had BROKEN the law without penalty.

"But he said unto them, have you not read what David did, when he was an hungered, and they that were with him; how he entered into the house of God, and did eat the Shewbread, which was not lawful for him but only for the priests?" (Matthew 12:3–4)

Christ's example to the Pharisees was one of law breaking, not law observance. Actually, David committed a serious infraction of the law of God. He and his companions entered the Tabernacle of God (and if this entry was into the Holy Place, even that entry was illegal). They also unlawfully ate the consecrated bread. David even committed this sin on the Sabbath day itself. Compare 1 Sam. 21:6 with Lev. 24:8. This is one of the reasons Christ used David's example of law-breaking in defense for His own disciples when they also violated the Sabbath rules.

Christ was telling the Pharisees that since David had broken the law on the Sabbath and without retribution, His disciples also had permission from Him to break the Sabbath law. David broke Temple laws, but Christ said, "In this place is one greater than the Temple" (Matthew 12:6). Christ was the One who created the Temple and the Sabbath in the first place. He was the One who formerly allowed David to break the Temple and Sabbath laws. And now Christ was commanding His disciples also to break the Sabbath laws. "For the Son of Man is Lord of the Sabbath" (verse 8). The Sabbath belonged to Christ. He was its Lord and could do with the Sabbath as He pleased. If Christ was the Son of God on earth (which He was), no one could hold Him accountable for doing with His own creation as He wished."[33]

What the Biblical examples show us is that it is very possible that when the designated Patriarchs entered the inner part of the Garden of Eden where God had His presence and where the tree of life existed, they would have been permitted to eat of the tree of life on that occasion if God would have allowed it. There is no text in Scriptures which forbids this possibility. On the contrary, we have given several examples which make this a distinct possibility.

While the evidence for eating of the tree of life to produce longevity in the Patriarchs mentioned in the Bible seems very possible, it is also possible that the longevity experienced by these certain individuals mentioned in the book of Genesis in particular did not involve eating from the tree of life. This will be the subject of the next chapter.

---

[33] E. Martin, Essentials of New Testament Doctrine, Ch. 20, ASK: Portland, OR, 2004.

8

They Walked With God

Up until this point in this book we have suggested the possibility that the Patriarchal longevity may have been caused by eating of the fruit the tree of life (the almond tree) due to certain individuals being permitted back into the Garden of Eden on an annual basis based upon the Biblical type of the High Priest entering the Holy of Holies on the Day of Atonement. The evidence for this possibility has been documented in our present research study.

While this is the case, we also must admit that there is another possibility which accounts for the longevity but that circumstance does not necessarily require the eating of the tree of life. Having said that, both of these suggestions go hand in hand in one way of looking at it because they involve certain personalities being able to return to the Garden of Eden and we are going to find that the Bible teaches that this happened to certain people.

The Bible shows that two personalities mentioned in the book of Genesis were able to return to the Garden of Eden and their stays in that area were extended for longer periods of time. Those two personalities were Enoch and Noah, both of whom are recorded in Scripture as having significant longevity well beyond what we experience today.

Enoch died before Noah so we will refer to his case first. The Bible mentions that he had a son, Methuselah, at age 65, and that after that he had other children and "walked with God 300 years." (Genesis 5:21,22)

We mention Enoch first also because there is a mistaken belief among many Bible believers concerning Enoch. Many believe that Enoch did not die like all other human beings die. Some Bible texts on the surface may seem to teach this idea. These are Genesis 5:24 and Hebrews 11:5, which say respectively:

"Enoch walked with God, and he was not, for God took him." (ESV)

"By faith Enoch was taken up so that he should not see death, and he was not found, because God had taken him. Now before he was taken he was commended as having pleased God." (ESV)

While the book of Genesis says that "Thus all the days of Enoch were 365 years." (Genesis 5:23 ESV), most Christians have come to believe that Enoch lived 365 years on earth and that after that he was transported to heaven where he still lives at the present time. On the surface, this is what the Bible seems to teach.

However, there are problems with this idea. The first concerns the simple fact that in Hebrews 11, St. Paul tells us the following happened to all of the individuals who he mentioned in that chapter saying:

"**These all died in faith**, not having received the things promised, but having seen them and greeted them from afar, and having acknowledged that they were strangers and exiles on the earth." Hebrew 11:13 ESV)

This text tells us that "These all died ...". This text appears well after v.5 which mentions Enoch, so it must be applied also to him. So, if Enoch was not taken to heaven or away from the earth and did not see dead in the traditional fashion, how do we explain these texts in Genesis and Hebrews which seem to show that he did not die?

Here we need a larger explanation to see what was taking place in the time when and near the time Enoch lived. According to the Biblical chronology, Enoch was born in year 622 after Adam and his 365th year would then be year 987. (Panino, Bible Chronology) Noah was born in 1056, which is only 69 years after the passing of Enoch.

We are told that "After Noah was 500 years old, Noah fathered Shem, Ham, and Japheth.." (Genesis 5:32 ESV) So, for 500 years of life, Noah did not have any children. In addition, we are told that 120 years before the Flood, the LORD made a decree that the Flood would be coming. (Genesis 6:3) This would have been year 1536 (*ibid.*, Panin) This would have been 20 years before Noah had his first son, who was Japhet in 1556. (*ibid.*, Panin)

What was taking place during this time period was that "The Nephilim were on the earth in those days, …" (Genesis 6:4 ESV) and "The Lord saw that the wickedness of man was great in the earth, and that every intention of the thoughts of his heart was only evil continually." (Genesis 6:5 ESV)

What we see is a situation of evil with only Noah being designated at this time as being one who "found favor in the eyes of the LORD." (Genesis 6:8 ESV) What we see in Noah is something similar to what we saw in Enoch because both of them were designated as individuals who "walked with God." (Gen. 5:21; 6:9)

Commentators point out what this phrase means on a practical level.

"Twice we are told (vv.22.24) that Enoch *walked with God* (*yithallek 'et-ha Elohim*), a description also applied to Noah in 6:9. This expression may be compared to *halak* (or *yithallek*) *lipne*, which indicates the service of a loyal servant, who goes before his master (sometimes human but mostly divine), paving the way, or who stands before his master ready to serve. Thus, Hezekiah walked before God (II Kings 20:3 par. Isaiah 38:3), as did the patriarchs. (Genesis 17:1; 24:40; 48:15) A bit more intimacy seems to be suggested by "walking with" as over against "walking before." "Walk with" captures an emphasis on communion and fellowship. In a number of passages, all addressed to a king or his dynasty, "to walk before God" strongly suggests obedience and subordination (I Kings 2:4; 3:6; 8:23, 25; 94), rather than worship and communion."[34]

So, Enoch, like Noah, "walked with God" meaning he had a close communion and fellowship with God. But what kind of "communion and fellowship" was it?

Most commentators concerning Enoch, however, believe that he departed this world and went to live in a heavenly existence with the LORD. This teaching is almost assumed by almost all people who read the Holy Scriptures.

"There is no further mention of Enoch in the Old Testament, but in Ecclesiasticus (49:14) he is brought forward as one of the peculiar glories of the Jews, as he was taken up from the earth. He pleased the LORD and was translated (Vulg. into Paradise), being a pattern of repentance.' (Ecclus. 44:14). In the Epistle to the Hebrews the spring and issue Enoch's life are clearly marked… 'By faith Enoch was translated ($\mu\epsilon\tau\epsilon\tau\dot{\epsilon}\theta\eta$) that he should not see death … for before his translation ($\mu\epsilon\tau\alpha\theta\dot{\epsilon}\sigma\epsilon\omega\varsigma$) he had this testimony, that he pleased God.' The contrast to this divine judgment is found in the constrained words of Josephus: 'Enoch departed to the Deity whence [the sacred writers] have not recorded his death.'

---

[34] Hamilton, Victor E. The New International Commentary on the Old Testament. The Book of Genesis – Chapters 1-17, William P. Eerdmans Publishing Co.; Grand Rapids: MI, 1990. p.258

(Ant. i,3,4) In the Epistle of Jude (v.14; comp. Enoch 60:8) he is described as "the seventh from Adam;" and the number is probably noticed as conveying the idea of divine completion and rest (comp. August c. Faust xii,14), while Enoch was himself a type of perfected humanity, "a man raised to heaven by pleasing God, while angels fell to earth by transgression" (Irenaeus, iv, 16, 2) Elijah was in like manner translated; and thus was the doctrine of immortality *palpably* taught under the ancient dispensation."[35]

This is the exact teaching about Enoch (and the prophet Elijah as well) that almost all Christians universally accept as the truth of the Bible.

What is unfortunate, however, is that most people who believe this teaching have not carefully looked at the whole counsel of God on this matter and have misinterpreted Scripture leaving out key facts in this whole matter of what happened to Enoch (and Elijah).

In this regard, I am going to refer to a quote given by my late father, which I think better captures the whole of the Scriptural account which concerns both Enoch and Elijah. This matter is also closely linked to the life of Noah, who, while he did not have the same experiences as Enoch and Elijah, what happened to him in regard to his "walking with God" was exactly the same thing as what happened

---

[35] M'cLintock and Strong, Cyclopedia of Biblical, Theological and Ecclesiastical Literature, Harper and Brothers Publishers, New York: 1883. Vol. III, pg. 224.

to Enoch. What we are going to find out is a whole new idea of what actually happened to especially Enoch (who is our prime subject here) and secondarily Elijah. Here is the quotation from my late father which present a new solution to this Biblical difficulty.

"Most Christians commonly assume that the Bible shows the prophets Enoch and Elijah as having been translated to heaven back in their times and that they are now living in an immortal state with Christ and God the Father (II Kings 2:1,11; Hebrews 11:5). The fact is, however, nothing could be farther from the truth. In no way do the Holy Scriptures teach that these two prophets are now immortal and in heaven."[36]

This quote really orients us in the right way to better understand what the Bible teaches about what happened to both Enoch and Elijah as well as their present reality and existence. The quote continues:

"It is the simplest thing in the world to show where the dead are at the present (both the righteous dead and the unrighteous dead) if one wants to rely solely on the teachings of the Holy Scriptures. They are presently in their graves

---

[36] Ernest Martin, 101 Bible Secrets Christians Do Not Know, ASK Publications: Portland: OR, 1993. Pgs. 109-111.

(thoroughly unconscious in every way) and they are awaiting the resurrection from the dead (see Ecclesiastes 9:5; Psalm 6:5; 146.4; John 3:13). The inspired revelation as to the state of the dead shows that they "sleep in the dust of the earth" (Daniel 12:2) and that none of them will "awake" from his or her death state until after the great tribulation at the end of the age (Daniel 12:1,2). For those who are "in Christ," they will be resurrected back to life when Christ Jesus returns with his saints (the angels) at his second advent (I Cor. 15:50-55; I Thess. 4:15-17). This is called "the first resurrection" (Rev. 20:5), and it is the plain teaching of Scripture. It solves so many problems to understand it." (*ibid.*)

We must, in my view, let the Scripture and its teachings on the current state of all dead people guide us in understanding what happened to Enoch and Elijah. This is particularly important and relevant to what we Christians believe about what happened to our Lord Jesus Christ and how He died for the sins of the world and was raised from the dead. We are talking about important and fundamental issues to the whole fabric of Christian teaching and we need to make sure that we are on solid Scriptural and theological grounds in what we believe. Continuing:

"Indeed, the only one who has ever lived in the flesh and has become an immortal being is Jesus Christ once he was resurrected from the dead. In fact, the apostle Paul in A.D. 63, over thirty years after Christ was resurrected from the dead,

58

stated that Christ was the one "who only hath immortality" (I Timothy 6:16). To state otherwise, as so many people are prone to do today, is to be totally inconsistent with scriptural truth and is a patent absurdity. Immortality for Christians will only arrive when Christ returns. It is only then that "this mortal must put on immorality" (I Corinthians 15:53). The false teaching of a "present immortality" in Christ (which is the belief that the soul is immortal or that there is a continual living existence of the human personality which transcends the physical consequences of death) is a teaching which makes a mockery out of the inspired revelation of God that the dead remain dead (and will continue to remain in their graves) until their resurrections from the dead." (*ibid.*)

The matter of who presently has immortality is not a minor one as far as the New Testament is concerned. It is fundamental to the very basis of the Christian message. It also goes back to the very beginning of the Bible's teaching in the book of Genesis about the necessity of mankind to seek eternal life outside of themselves.

"And let's face it, if mankind were created by God with an inherent immortality, then the "tree of life" in the midst of the Garden of Eden would have been a redundant item in the Garden. The first lie of the serpent was to tell Eve and Adam that God was a liar and that they would never die (Genesis 3:4). The serpent was trying to convince Eve that it was not necessary to take of the "tree of life" to attain an immortality because, according to the serpent, they had immortality already. He said: "Ye shall not surely die." Satan has been a liar from the very beginning (John 8:44) and he and his ministers (II Cor. 11:14,15) are constantly perpetuating the same lie to human beings that "ye shall not surely die." At the present, however, some preachers are slightly modifying the serpent's teaching by saying that if you are "in Christ" then you are presently immortal and that you don't have to wait for salvation which is in accord with the scriptural teaching concerning the resurrection from the dead which will occur at Christ's advent. It is erroneous to say that Christians are immortal already. Nothing could be more wrong." (*ibid*.)

With this solid Scriptural foundation in mind, we can now really look more carefully at the question at hand concerning Enoch and Elijah and what really happened to both of them. We begin with the question about Elijah.

"But what about Enoch and Elijah? Do we not read in the Scripture that Enoch did not die and that Elijah was transported into heaven? Let us first look at the matter of Elijah. The verse that makes some people think that Elijah was taken into heaven where God lives is II Kings 2:11. This describes the scene when Elijah departed from his successor Elisha. It says: "And it came to pass, as they still went on and talked, that, behold, there appeared a chariot of fire, and horses of fire, and parted them both asunder; and Elijah went up by a whirlwind into heaven." From this, it has been surmised by many people that Elijah was taken to God's throne in heaven and has remained there alive ever since. In no way is this true.

The fact is, there are three usages of the word "heaven" in the Bible. One is where the birds fly and the clouds exist (that is, our atmosphere) (Genesis 1:20). The second is where all the heavenly bodies are (Genesis 1:14-17). And the third is, indeed, the very region where God himself resides. This is even called "the third heaven" by apostle Paul (II Corinthians 12:1,2). Was it "the third heaven" into which Elijah was taken? The answer is clearly NO. We even have the express teaching of Christ himself that no one (man or woman) has ever ascended into the heaven where God besides. "And no man hath ascended up to heaven, but he that came down from heaven" (John 3:13). This means that Elijah (who lived almost 900 years before the birth of Christ) could not have gone into the heaven in which God has his residence. He simply went upwards into the heavens where the birds fly and the clouds exist and was transferred to another location on earth.

Such a circumstance concerning Elijah was even anticipated by those who lived in Elijah's time and knew him personally. A righteous man by the name of Obadiah told Elijah that he believed God would cause "the Spirit of YHVH to carry thee whither I know not where" (I Kings 18:12). This shows that the power of Elijah to be transported by the Spirit from one place on earth to another was already recognized as possible by the people who lived at the time. And when Elijah handed over power to his successor, Elisha, he was indeed transported through the air out of the central area of Palestine into the kingdom of Judah in the south (II Kings 2:11). Elijah only went into the "first heaven" (the atmosphere of the earth), and not into outer space or the heaven of God's throne. This is made clear in the Scripture because about seven years later we find Elijah still on earth (but this time living in Judah) writing a letter to the King of Judah (II Chronicles 21:12). So Elijah continued to live on earth.

Elijah was simply taken miraculously through the air to a location in southern Judah. The prophet Ezekiel experienced the same phenomenon in his day (Ezekiel 3:12-14) and even the evangelist Philip was similarly transported bodily through the air from a spot near Gaza to the city of Azotus a few miles away (Acts 8:39,40). Thus, Elijah was not taken to the heaven where God lived. The prophet died a few years after his "transfer" and is awaiting his resurrection from the dead (like all the saints of old). Of all who have lived in the flesh, Christ "only hath immortality" (I Timothy 6:16)." (*ibid.*)

This makes perfect sense and is based on sound Biblical reasoning and a solid Scriptural basis. Now, let us consider the matter of what happened to Enoch.

"Now what about Enoch? The answer is much the same. The apostle Paul in the Book of Hebrews says this about Enoch: "By faith Enoch was translated [Greek: transferred] that he should not see death; and was not found because God had translated [transferred] him: for before his translation he had this testimony that he pleased God" (Hebrews 11:5). Notice that Paul did not say Enoch did not die. He simply said he was transferred by God to a place where no death could be seen. Where was that place? The answer is plain but it may be a surprise to some people. Enoch was transferred into the Garden of Eden which remained on earth until the Flood. This was the place where God had His presence (Genesis 3:8; 4:16). This was a place where anyone taken into the Garden could talk to God face to face as the word "presence" signifies.

It was in the Garden that God was accustomed to walk in the cool of the day (Genesis 3:8). Now note this point. The Scripture says that two men were able to "walk WITH GOD" and these were Enoch and Noah (Genesis 5:22-24; 6:9), while later men such as Abraham were able to "walk BEFORE GOD" (Genesis 17:1). It was only "in the midst of the Garden" that God walked, and to "walk with God" meant that Enoch was transferred into the Garden where he stayed in a permanent way in God's presence until his death. Noah was also permitted to "walk with God" in the Garden in Eden, but he was also allowed to leave in order to build the ark.

63

Thus, Enoch at the age of 365 was not found in human society any longer. As the Scripture says: "He was not; for God took him [transferred him into the Garden]," where, as Paul said, "he should not see death" (Hebrews 11:5). Paul was not saying that Enoch would not die. He simply meant that Enoch was taken to a place where no death could be seen. And while in the Garden no death was seen. The same occurs in the New Jerusalem where it says "there shall be no more death" (Revelation 21:4). But Enoch did die (maybe near the time when the Garden ceased at the Flood) because Paul said "these ALL DIED" (Hebrews 11:13), and this obviously (as the context shows) including Enoch. This means that both Enoch and Elijah are like all other men. Both are dead and awaiting the resurrection at the second advent of Christ."[37]

So, what we find is that certain individuals in the Patriarchal period enjoyed an existence which still allowed a much closer communion with God in His Garden, a place where death was not in evidence like other places and being in this environment in close proximity to God and His presence could have directly affected these Patriarchs who were allowed to experience this reality.

---

[37] Ernest Martin, 101 Bible Secrets Christians Do Not Know, ASK Publications: Portland: OR, 1993. Pgs. 109-111.

9

The Full and Complete Destruction of the Garden of Eden Ends the Earlier Instances of Extreme Patriarchal Longevity

One of the most interesting subjects in the Bible is that of the Flood of Noah. This event is really a mystery to many people about the details of how it happened. No doubt, people are really interested in this issue. If you do any research at all, you will find hundreds of opinions on the Flood and how it happened and these opinions will cover a whole range of different opinions. Numerous books, articles and websites are devoted to this important issue.

The focus of this chapter is the verse: "And the waters assuaged." (Genesis 8:1) So let's talk about this seemingly unimportant passage because it is in this passage that much interesting information is contained.

Honestly, when we study Genesis or other sections of the Bible where we have very little information, we have to take what we do have seriously and look very carefully and closely at the information provided and do our best to understand what it meant to the writer who wrote it, who in this case was Moses. We want to know the meaning that Moses wished to convey if we can.

We in the modern world have been influenced wrongly by epic films and artistic depictions about biblical subjects concerning many issues including the Flood

Now, what difference does it make? The point is, films (and by extension photographs, television and paintings) influence dramatically people's opinions about all kinds of things and the Bible is no exception. Look at the Hollywood films about the Flood. They seemingly follow the Biblical narrative and you see people climbing up to the tops of mountains to escape the Flood; you see the ark floating on huge oceans of water and torrential downpours; you see rain for forty days and forty nights; you see the water covering the tops of the mountains and so on. However, are these really accurate descriptions? According to Hollywood, yes; but according to the Bible, no!

However, there is one verse which I am focusing on in this chapter which seems to indicate this idea pretty clearly. It is the following which are the last few words of the passage in question: "And the waters assuaged." (Gen. 8:1)

When you read this passage, you get the feeling that the waters that were submerging the whole mountains were somehow miraculously removed from the earth by a divine agency. This is what you feel on the surface when you read the last section of Genesis 7 and the first verse of Genesis 8. It seems so clear that this is what it means. But is it?

When we look at the Hebrew word for "assuaged" which is ישכו- *yascu*, this word needs some defining. Yes, it can mean "assuaged" or "receded," however in this context many ancient commentators point out something else.

Rabbi Raphael Hirschinson in his excellent commentary on Genesis says the following: " וישכו– *vayascu* (root שכך) The use of this expression indicates that the action of the water of the flood was not merely mechanically destructive but also chemically dissolving. According to one remark in Sanhedrin 108b (quoting here from the Babylonian Talmud – one of the ancient authoritative works on Jewish law and Bible interpretation – see http://www.come-and-hear.com/sanhedrin/sanhedrin_108.html), they were רותחין, seething. שכך is the reverse of boiling and bubbling up of a torrent." (pg. 155). Continuing, Rabbi Hirschinson shows that to understand this verse it is essential to refer to a passage in the book of Esther chapter 7, verse 10, which says:

"Then the king's wrath was pacified."

The word for "pacified" in Esther 7:10 and the word for "assuaged" in Genesis 8:1 come from the same root. The point that arises out of these passages when we begin to dig deeper is that the Floodwaters themselves were boiling hot. Rabbi Hirschinson references a key passage in the Babylonian Talmud in this regard and it is good to show here what those ancient commentaries said about this verse. Note if here:

R. Hisda said: With hot passion they sinned (speaking about those in the pre-Flood period), and by hot water they were punished. [For] here it is written, And the water cooled; (Genesis 8:1) whilst elsewhere it is said, Then the king's wrath cooled down. (Esther 7:10) (Babylonian Talmud, Sanhedrin 108b)

You can see that this ancient commentator clearly understood that the waters of the Flood were hot water and he even translated the word as "cooled." When we think about it, depending on our perspective, it could very easily mean that the waters indeed "cooled off" rather than "assuaged" or "run off" from a higher point to a lower point. What we find here is that those individuals who translated the word "assuaged" may have been influenced by their opinion of what took place in the Flood through means other than looking at the ancient sources (like religious art, paintings in churches, stained glass windows or icons) and comparing the information we find in the Biblical texts.

Hot water during the Flood? Yes. In fact, we have many ancient nations producing Flood type narratives and "a Finnish story of the Deluge (the Flood) is of hot water." (Hastings: Encyclopedia of Religion and Ethics, vol. IV, p. 548)

What has to be understood is the whole conception of what took place in the Flood needs to be reexamined. Even the word for "flood" (מבול - mabul) does not always specifically mean "flood." Note that in passages in the New Testament where the Flood is referenced, the Greek word used is kataklusmos (kataklusmos), from which we get the English word *cataclysm* or *cataclysmic*. The point is, while all floods to one degree or another can be cataclysmic in effect, not all *cataclysmic* events are necessarily floods. It is important to note that the Hebrew word (מבול - *mabul*) only appears in the Hebrew Bible 12 times, 11 of which are in the first eleven chapters of Genesis. (the remaining time is in Psalm 29:10) We even find in the first passage where this word in referenced that the Lord says: "I do bring a flood (מבול - *mabul* – "a cataclysmic event") of waters ..." (Genesis 6:17) It seems to indicate that to limit the description of this event to that of a "flood" is to miss the intent and power of this word. What took place in the early chapters of Genesis was a complete destruction of everything alive on earth and it looks like that while water was involved, that water was not only very hot, but that it also had corrosive qualities to it.

What this information shows us is that the Garden of Eden suffered a complete destruction at the time of this cataclysmic flood event and that after that the ages of the Patriarchs began to be reduced to the age of human beings that we today are familiar with.

10

Final Thoughts

One point I did wish to make is that some of the things we are discussing here are esoteric and very symbolic. Having said that, I believe they are still relevant. In fact, the whole of the Gospel message of Christ Jesus has very strong symbolism associated with it.

While some teachings in the Bible are mysterious or their details are not clear on the surface, this is not a reason not to investigate them and attempt to learn what the LORD was really teaching. On the contrary, the Bible is full of secrets and many of these secrets await our discovery if we keep our minds open to the Bible and its teachings. As Deuteronomy 29:29 tells us: "The secret things belong to the LORD our God: …" In addition, we note in the book of Proverbs (or Parables) a teaching about the "dark sayings of the LORD" (Proverbs 1:6) and finally we see in Psalm 78:2 the following statement talking about parabolic teachings similar to those given by Christ: "I will open my mouth in a parable: I will utter dark sayings of old." Yes, the Bible has secret teachings in it. It is just up to us to search them out and learn new truths.

One additional thing that I think it is important to close on is the fact that this whole issue will no longer be relevant to us who are resurrected from the dead when our Lord, Jesus Christ returns. No! We will no longer be mortal at that time and we will not need to eat anything at that time to keep us alive for longer periods. But, we will be changed into immortal beings at that time as St. Paul mentioned (1 Corinthians 15:51-57). May God speed that day.

APPENDIX I

Quote Showing the Location of the Land of Eden and the Garden from "Solving the Riddle of Noah's Flood" by Ernest L. Martin

"With these geographical indications of Moses in mind, it becomes rather easy to identify the location of the Land of Eden, as well as the Garden and even the two mysterious rivers called the Pison and the Gihon. Since we are told that the Euphrates and the Tigris were two of the four rivers that came together to form the source of the one large river that debouched into the Persian Gulf, then the Land of Eden had to have (as its southern boundary) the coastal region of the Persian Gulf.

Even the early Mesopotamian records (discovered at Nippur in southern Babylon about 70 years ago) describe a place called Dilmun that resembled the biblical description of the Garden in Eden. The New Bible Dictionary (article Eden) said the tablets showed this area as a pleasant place in which neither sickness nor death were known. It was called "the land of the living" and the home of the immortals. This sea was located near the head of the Persian Gulf. Other records show a sacred tree in the area. The similarities between this Mesopotamian notion of an earthly paradise and the biblical Eden has prompted some scholars to conclude that the Genesis account depends upon the

Mesopotamian stories. Whatever the case, this "paradise" was located around the northern end of the Persian Gulf Remarkably, this is precisely where Moses said his four rivers came together (at the Garden) to form the source of the one river that exited into the Persian Gulf.

All of this is easily determined if one realizes that Moses was giving directions about his river system going upstream, not downstream! This proper understanding of what Moses meant can now help us in identifying the two mysterious rivers (the Pison and the Gihon) which have given commentators so much trouble in locating. Since two of the rivers which came together in the Garden region of Eden were the Euphrates and the Tigris, then the Pison and the Gihon also had to enter the Garden in this same general area. Moses said both rivers had "circuitous" courses which flowed through all parts of two geographical areas that were large in extent (Gen. 2:11,13). Interestingly, there are (even today) two such rivers that precisely fit the description of Moses.

Let us look at the first river that Moses mentioned. It was the Pison. He said it encompassed (in a circuitous fashion) all the land of Havilah. Just where was Havilah? This is pretty easy to identify. In the Bible is the phrase "from Havilah to Shur" (Gen.25:18). Since the phrase has the ring of describing an "A to Z" geographical swing (that is, from one extreme point to another), then Havilah has to be in the opposite direction from Shur. It is well known that Shur was a district near Egypt and the Red Sea. Havilah, then, was located in an opposite direction from Shur.

This means that Havilah was in the distant east from Shur. This would place it at the northern end of the Persian Gulf. And indeed, the early classical geographer, Eratosthenes (quoted by Strabo), located the (C)Havlotaioi (which certainly appears to be a Greek rendition of the word Havilah) in an area just to the north of the Persian Gulf (M'Clintock and Strong, vol. IV, p. 100). This would place the people of Havilah (and the area of Havilah itself) somewhat eastward from southern Babylonia and reaching into the Persian highlands. And what do we find coming from that region? There is a river flowing from that large area into the Euphrates/Tigris river system (in southern Mesopotamia) that is "circuitous" in its course just as Moses stated. It is today called the Karun (which has a major tributary named the Khersan). The earlier name for this river must have been the Pison that Moses talked about.

The other river mentioned by Moses was the Gihon. It was also "circuitous" and encompassed all the land of Cush (Gen.2:13). And true to what Moses said, just to the north and east of Babylon were the mountains of the Cassites (mentioned in early Mesopotamian records certainly representing the Cushites). This river also flowed into the Euphrates/Tigris river system in southern Mesopotamia just as Moses stated. It is today called the Karkheh.

All these four rivers flow together (or once flowed together) to form the one major river mentioned by Moses that finally debouched into the Persian Gulf. We will show later that before the flood of Noah, this one major river that left the Garden (formed by the four tributaries) flowed many more miles south and eastward than it does today before it entered the Persian Gulf because (as this booklet will show) the level of the Gulf was lower by about 30 feet before the flood (as were all ocean levels).

What we find in this geographical description given by Moses is a perfectly proper account that people in the fifteenth century B.C. would have understood without difficulty. Moses simply gave his description of the location of Eden by starting at the head of the river (at its mouth where it debouched into the Persian Gulf) and then he proceeded upstream to the Garden where the river divided into four heads. From the Garden he continued his description of the rivers by informing the Israelites about the mountainous regions to the east and north of the Land of Eden from whence three of the rivers came. He had to give more details about the Pison and the Gihon because they were smaller rivers and encompassed lands to the east of Mesopotamia which were unfamiliar to the Israelites. He gave no detailed information about the course of the Euphrates because the Israelites would have known all about that river already. (pgs. 12-14)

Other books by Samuel Martin

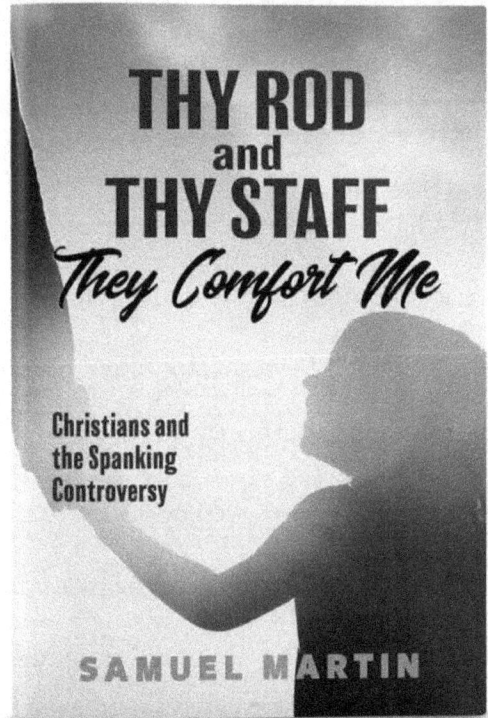

Thy Rod and Thy Staff, They Comfort Me: Christians and the Spanking Controversy – Available free here in soft copy – www.biblechild.com or on Amazon in hard copy – https://www.amazon.com/gp/product/0978533909/ref=dbs_a_def_rwt_bibl_vppi_i1

Reviews of the book

Thy Rod and Thy Staff, They Comfort Me:

Christians and the Spanking Controversy

"I've had a chance to read through your manuscript and I find it very interesting! I think you've made an important contribution, especially to contextualizing biblical ideas about childrearing. I hope you will find a publisher for this book. I'm sure many others would benefit from learning of your research."

Dr. Dawn Devries, John Newton Thomas Professor of Systematic Theology, Union Theological Seminary, USA and contributor to the ground breaking volume "The Child in Christian Thought" (Eerdmans: 2000)

"This is not an easy read, but it is one any Christian who desires to be true to the Bible in the first instance should take time to read. ... In my view this study is a definitive reading of the biblical texts for Christians and non-Christians alike."

Rev. Alistair McBride, Scots Presbyterian Church – Hamilton, New Zealand (see www.repeal59.blogspot.com - July 25 2006)

"Many thanks for sending me a copy of your book. Since I, like so many, cannot read Hebrew, I found your analysis of language fascinating and persuasive. Your exploration of these complex issues is thorough and convincing"

Dr. Philip Greven, Professor Emeritus, Rutgers University, author of "Spare the Child: The Religious Roots of Punishment and the Psychological Impact of Physical Abuse" (Random House, 1992)

"These and other verses, as well as the overall teaching about disciplining children in the Bible is ably discussed by Jerusalem-based Christian biblical scholar Samuel Martin, who has produced a wonderful book, Thy Rod and Thy Staff They Comfort Me: Christians and the Spanking Controversy, available as a free PDF download here with no cost or obligation. Martin has been joined by a significant number of other informed Christian scholars and commentators who are questioning the both the traditional translation and interpretation of these overly quoted verses from the book of Proverbs. I recommend Martin's work for those biblically oriented folk out there who have wondered about what the Bible really says regarding using corporeal punishment of any kind to discipline children—or for that matter anyone who wants to be more informed on this controversial topic."

Professor James D. Tabor, Chair (2004-2014) of the Department of Religious Studies at the University of North Carolina, where he has taught since 1989. He is currently Professor of ancient Judaism and early Christianity.

"I want to take my hat off to Samuel Martin and say, Thanks!

When I think about Samuel Martin, what comes to mind is a contemporary and contextualized, this-world version of William Wilberforce. He certainly has Wilberforce blood running through his veins. He is a Christian living in Jerusalem with an interest in connecting to the rest of the world in ways that are helpful and strategic about how to live out one's faith. Check his website: samuelmartin.blogspot.com. You will find interesting discussions about various biblical subjects.

In addition to being a blogger, Samuel is an author. I just finished reading his book Thy Rod and Thy Staff They Comfort Me: Christians and the Spanking Controversy. I ordered the book from a California source and had it delivered to a Canadian residence http://www.archivescalifornia.com/. Unlike more academic books that I tend to write, which can often be inaccessible to average readers (!), Samuel Martin does a good job of writing with an easy-to-understand touch. For me the greatest benefit in reading his book was to see how a movement towards an anti-spanking position can be developed through Jewish sources and readings of Scripture (as well as Christian ones). He comes to similar conclusions that I do regarding the spanking controversy but his path through the biblical material is quite different - a fascinating read.

Blogger, author and, most importantly, activist! My third thanks to Samuel is that he has reminded me of my own need to be at least to some extent . . . an activist. He has not done this by way of harassment. No, he has shown me this through his own life and example. He would be happy to know that recently I have broken out of my insulated scholarly circles and actually done a handful of radio interviews. Now that is a stretch for a stuffy, old professor of New Testament. Through his own activist work quite extensive as I have watched from afar he is changing the world one person at a time. He does so often by putting people together in ways that help to bring influence on those who perhaps would otherwise not listen. Samuel has reminded me of something that is easily forgotten in the ivory towers of academia, namely, that ideas only work to the degree that there are people willing to influence (other) people about those ideas. So, on three accounts my hat is off to Samuel Martin - blogger, author and activist." - Professor William Webb

Dr. Bill Webb is Adjunct Professor of Biblical Studies at Tyndale Seminary. He has worked as a pastor, chaplain, and professor over a span of over twenty years. In addition to conference speaking ministry, he has published several articles and books, including Returning Home (Sheffield Press, 1993), Slaves, Women, and Homosexuals (IVP, 2001), Discovering Biblical Equality (two chapters; IVP, 2005), Four Views on Moving from the Bible to Theology (one view and responses; Zondervan, 2009), Corporal Punishment in the Bible: A Redemptive Hermeneutic for Troubling Texts (IVP, 2011).

Other books by Samuel Martin

THY ROD and THY STAFF
They Comfort Me BOOK II

14 years in the making, Samuel Martin returns with his second volume in the series, "Thy Rod and Thy Staff, They Comfort Me," further strengthening an already compelling case against corporal punishment in this new book, focused on the New Testament book of Hebrews chapter 12:5-11, which is a key text quoted by many Christians today in their belief in corporal punishment.

FEATURES OF THIS NEW BOOK ARE:
- The original manuscript order of Hebrews and its importance?
- Who wrote Hebrews and why that is important?
- If Paul wrote Hebrews, why did he not identify himself openly?
- What geographical region was Hebrews written to?
- When was the book of Hebrews written?
- What is the main subject of the book of Hebrews?
- Who is the book of Hebrews relevant for today?
- How does this survey of Hebrews link to our understanding of the debate concerning spanking children in the 21st century?

The first book in the series, 'Thy Rod and Thy Staff, They Comfort Me: Christians and the Spanking Controversy,' (published in 2006) was not sold, but has been available as a free download on numerous sites on the web and through www.biblechild.com. A printed version is now also available for purchase through Amazon.

THY ROD
and
THY STAFF
They Comfort Me
BOOK II

The Book of Hebrews and the Corporal Punishment of Children in the Christian Context

SAMUEL MARTIN

Thy Rod and Thy Staff, They Comfort Me: Book II – The Book of Hebrews and the Corporal Punishment of Children in the Christian Context – Available on Amazon in hard copy.

https://www.amazon.com/Samuel-Martin/e/B00HP94ZZA/ref=dp_byline_cont_pop_book_1

Reviews of the book

Thy Rod and Thy Staff, They Comfort Me: Book II

The Book of Hebrews and the Corporal

Punishment of Children in the Christian Context

"Samuel Martin does a good job of writing with an easy to understand touch ... He comes to similar conclusions that I do regarding the spanking controversy."

- Professor William Webb, Adjunct Professor of Biblical Studies, Tyndale Seminary, Canada and author of the book "Corporal Punishment in the Bible: A Redemptive Movement Hermeneutic for Troubling Texts" (InterVarsity, 2011)

"I think you present a well-crafted argument."

Pastor Crystal Lutton, author of "Biblical Parenting"

"a very provocative and stimulating perspective of Hebrews."

Clay Clarkson, author of "Heartfelt Discipline: Following God's Path of Life to the Heart of Your Child."

Other books by Samuel Martin

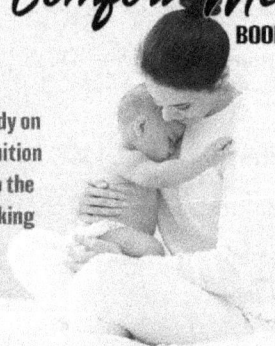

THY ROD and THY STAFF
They Comfort Me BOOK III

10 years in the making, Samuel Martin returns with his third volume in the series, *"Thy Rod and Thy Staff, They Comfort Me,"* responding to an urgent need in Christ's Body to address the falsehoods Christian mothers have been told with regard to their God-given maternal intuition.

Christian mothers have been told:
- You are flawed
- You are dirty and need to be cleaned up
- Your heart is full of evil and needs to be ignored and suppressed
- There is nothing good inside you
- Yuo cannot trust yourself and your God-given intuition and maternal leadings
- you are "too sensitive" and that is bad
- What you think you "just know" is wrong and almost certainly not from God
- Do not ever trust your feelings. They are wrong and against God. If you listen to your own feelings, you will be embrracing evil

This book seeks to support Christian mothers as they reconnect with their holy, God-given intuition to help them feel at peace in their body, heart, and soul.

"Samuel Martin does a good job of writing with an easy-to-understand touch... He comes to similar conclusions that I do regarding the spanking controversy."
- Professor William Webb, Adjunct Professor of Biblical Studies, Tyndale Seminary, Canada, and author of *Corporal Punishment in the Bible: A Redemptive-Movement Hermeneutic for Troubling Texts* (InterVarsity, 2011)

"I think you present a well-crafted argument."
- Pastor Crystal Lutton, author of *Biblical Parenting*

"...a very provocative and stimulating perspective of Hebrews."
- Clay Clarkson, author of *Heartfelt Discipline: Following God's Path of Life to the Heart of Your Child*

The first books in the series, *Thy Rod and Thy Staff, They Comfort Me* series.

Thy Rod and Thy Staff, They Comfort Me: Book III – A Biblical Study on Maternal Intuition and its link to the Issue of Spanking Children – Available on Amazon in hard copy.

https://www.amazon.com/Samuel-Martin/e/B00HP94ZZA/ref=dp_byline_cont_pop_book_1

Reviews of the book

Thy Rod and Thy Staff, They Comfort Me: Book III

A Biblical Study on Maternal Intuition and its link

to the Issue of Spanking Children

"Samuel Martin has been so helpful - breaking down scripture and historical context as it applies to living and mothering today, so in spite of my biases, I picked up this next book from him.

The reason for this book is the reason I was hesitant. I, too, was raised to never trust my own intuition or instincts. Having read this book, I see now how flawed that teaching is. Does Christ not redeem the whole person?

For me, this book has been very affirming and healing. Ignoring my intuition as "always flawed" has landed me in some very dangerous situations. I wish I had read this long ago. But I'm grateful for it now.

Not only for this affirmation and deeper understanding of what scripture says, but also for being built up spiritually - maturing and being able to parse the teaching of men from the teaching of scripture." – Christina Dronen, https://gentlechristianparenting.com/

"Samuel Martin's first Thy Rod and thy Staff book was the first gentle parenting book I read and it was like a breath of fresh air. I've always felt like there was something wrong with so many Christians using scriptures to say that the Bible tells us to spank. When I came across that book everything made so much sense. Samuel Martin is very thorough and explains things from a biblical perspective in great detail. This book has been a huge blessing as well and it has made me feel more confident in following those God given instincts as a wife and mother. May God bless the Author and may God bless others with the teachings in this book!" – Debbie Donisa, Amazon Review

Other books by Samuel Martin

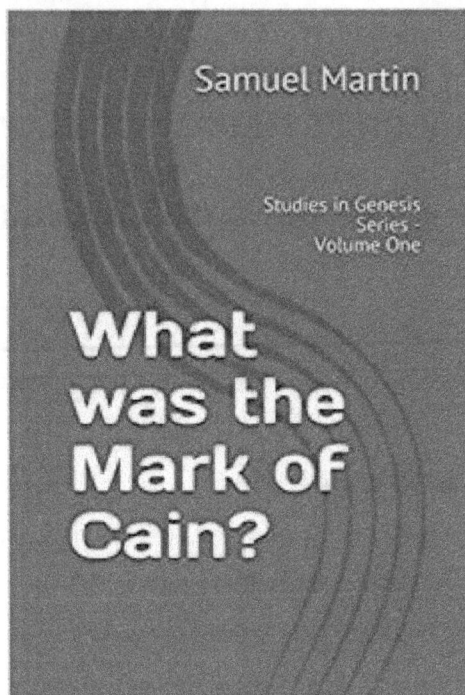

What was the Mark of Cain? Scholars and lay people alike have been asking this question for centuries. In this new book, Samuel Martin proposes a new idea to help answer this age-old question. This new book stresses the following points in seeking to identify what was the Mark of Cain:

- ✓ The early narratives in Genesis cannot be understood properly without an appreciation of the fact that these narratives have very strong symbolic teachings associated with them relating to the Holy Temple
- ✓ Solid comparative studies of the specific texts in Genesis relating to this story with other Biblical passages will pay great dividends in helping to understand what the Mark of Cain was
- ✓ In this book, we propose a number of interesting and thought provoking suggestions about Cain and Abel age's at the time when Abel died
- ✓ A new proposal concerning the Biblical translation of the "Land of Nod."

This book is available on Amazon at the following link:

www.amazon.com/Samuel-Martin/e/B00HP94ZZA/ref=dp_byline_cont_pop_book_1

Testimonies from Christian moms about the book Thy Rod and Thy Staff, They Comfort Me: Christians and the Spanking Controversy

"Wow! I'm so glad that you have been able to give this book out to so many. [over 400 in the last 12 months] I still am so grateful that I discovered it. It has helped us to parent each of our children with love and respect. We have recently become foster parents and I was so proud to be able to say that we were Christians who don't spank. They make foster parents sign a contract to not spank foster children if they use corporal punishment with their own children. They are so used to Christians spanking there own children and seemed surprised that we didn't. Blessing to you and all the work that you do."

"I would very much appreciate a PDF copy of your book "Thy Rod and Thy Staff, They Comfort Me; Christians and the Spanking Controversy".

"Well since then I married and brought up two daughters. In the [mentions denomination] culture of the time, under pressure from the ministry, I did apply a limited amount of spanking with my elder daughter for a very few years, but by the time my second daughter was born I had come to the view that this was not a Christian way to bring up a child, and neither daughter was spanked from then on.

My daughters are now two fine, loving adult ladies. My eldest daughter is now married, and has a two-year-old son, and a three-week-old daughter.

She too is now concerned to bring up her children in a correct way, but is also aware of some pressure on her to apply spanking, which she has thus far resisted."

"Hello, I am a Christian, expecting my first child in August. I am floored by the willingness of many Christians to twist the Word of God so horribly. I look forward to having this book as a tool to back up what I already believe about parenting with the grace God parents us."

"I am a new mom to a beautiful baby girl and have recently found your blog! I was hoping to get a copy of your book, Thy Rod and Thy Staff, They Comfort Me. I was spanked as a child and always thought that was what God wanted but THANK JESUS for the many revelations I have had recently about parenting! I just feel so genuinely excited about raising my daughter now...thinking God expected / wanted me to hit my kids to teach them right always felt wrong to me but I was prepared to do it because I really believed that to be what God wanted. I'm so grateful my eyes have been opened. And so looking forward to educating myself more on this issue. Thank you for what you do!!! You are a blessing."

"Hello! I am so excited about your book. The biblical spanking issue is one I feel God has put on my heart since childhood, as I was spanked and have vivid memories of it. Where many have forgotten the child's perspective with spankings, I remember them well and with much pain."

"I'd love to read a copy of your book. My husband and I were both abused and while we choose not to spank, we have hit our children in anger in the past. As we have worked on our abuse issues and grown closer to God, it has gotten easier to take a moment and not react out of anger.

Our children's guidance counselor gave a class on Love and Logic and that also really helped.

One of my friends shared your status on Facebook today. I shared it after reading the discussion left in the comments of that status. I thought you'd be interested in what I posted:

This is great. I think it's pretty sad that people are using this status to argue that hitting a child is necessary. How else do you discipline? Consequences, removal, distraction...all depending on the situation and age of the child.

We get disciplined at work and in society without hitting. In fact, we're told hitting and bullying is wrong. Yet we think kids are too stupid to learn without hitting...while being smart enough to understand that hitting from a caregiver is different?"

"I am in full support and am still so extremely thankful for your book. It has given me such resolve and a sense of peace in what I am doing with my daughter. I am indeed treading in new water, as far as my own family is concerned, but I'm also blazing a path to be seen, and hopefully, someday emulated by fellow family, as I go. My family will be the evidence that it can be done by someone with little experience in gentle rearing, but a determination given and confirmed by God Himself. I want to thank you so much for your work. I plan on passing it on to anyone who will listen."

"Yes, thanks. I was tremendously blessed [by your book]. I even went through it with my Pastor, who of course, is old school and is moderately pro-spanking, like most Christians. It challenged him, but did not convince him completely. It's really hard to get through to people who are so ingrained to spanking. But it did make him think and question many things, so I'm going to continue to work on him, and hopefully the Holy Spirit will enlighten him.

It's amazing to see what a strong hold "tradition" has on people because exegetically and logically, I don't see the proof for spanking. My Pastor was even a little taken back because he couldn't find exegeses from any of his commentaries on the "spanking" passages. It seems like it's just been taken for granted over all these years. Thanks for you all your hard work!"

About the Author

Samuel Martin was born in England and is the youngest child of Dr. Ernest L. and Helen R. Martin, who are both Americans and natives of the state of Oklahoma.

He lived in the UK for the first seven years of his life before moving to the USA with his family. He lived in the USA until 2001 when he married a native Israeli Christian and relocated to live in Jerusalem, where he currently resides.

He and his wife, Sonia, have two daughters.

His experience with biblical scholarship began at an early age. His father lead a program in conjunction with Hebrew University and the late Professor Benjamin Mazar, where over a five year period, some 450 college students came to work on an archaeological excavation in Jerusalem starting in 1969.

Since that first trip, Samuel has visited Israel on 14 different occasions living more than 19 years of his life in the country. He has toured all areas of Israel as well as worked in several archaeological excavations.

He writes regularly on biblical subjects with a particular interest in children, families, nature, science, the Bible, and gender in the Biblical context. He holds an MA from the University of the Holy Land in Inter-Cultural Studies and the Bible.

Website: www.biblechild.com
Contact: info@biblechild.com
Facebook: https://www.facebook.com/byblechyld/
Blog: www.samuelmartin.blogspot.com
Amazon: https://www.amazon.com/Samuel-Martin/e/B00HP94ZZA/ref=dp byline cont book 1

www.ingramcontent.com/pod-product-compliance
Lightning Source LLC
Chambersburg PA
CBHW021137020426
42331CB00005B/812